C000217283

POCKET BOOK OF
ONE-LINERS

BRUSQUE
BRUSH-OFFS

ALLSORTED.

An exclusive edition for

for all your gift books and gift stationery

This edition first published in Great Britain in 2017
by Allsorted Ltd, Watford, Herts, UK WD19 4BG

© Susanna Geoghegan Gift Publishing

Author: Roffy
Cover design: Milestone Creative
Contents layout: seagulls.net

ISBN: 978-1-910562-93-2

Printed in China

CONTENTS

INTRODUCTION

The best brush-off will stop an adversarial in their tracks. Their argument in pieces, their question repelled or their drama belittled. The brush-er victorious, the brush-ee vanquished.

You see it all the time in the movies. Whatever the situation, the hero drops a killer one-liner like a bomb. Mic drop. Exit.

But that's not real life. The scriptwriter spent hours crafting the perfect retort. And don't forget that they also wrote the set-up line in the first place.

Unfortunately, life hasn't provided you with a pause button and a team of scriptwriters. On the bright side, it has provided you with this book.

Across these pages you will find all kinds of brush-offs, comebacks, retorts and dismissals. Wherever you are, whatever you're up to, there's a one-liner here that will disarm your conversational combatant.

Just remember that microphones are expensive – try not to break it when you drop it.

LOVE ON THE ROCKS

FINDING 'THE ONE' IS A BIG CHALLENGE IN LIFE. WHILE THERE MAY BE PLENTY OF FISH IN THE SEA, IF YOU CAST YOUR NET TOO WIDE THERE WILL BE PLENTY YOU NEED TO TOSS OUT OF YOUR NET.

'We both know it's not working out', 'It's not you, it's me' and 'I'm actually a hologram' are the most common phrases that signal the end of a relationship in a sympathetic, understanding way. The pair of you gave it your best shot, and you wish each other well.

But there are some occasions when a fond farewell just isn't right. There's been point-scoring along the way and the right parting shot will win big.

Whether you've barely met, spent an evening together or have dated for a while, these brush-offs are going to draw the line under the relationship in thick red ink.

COME-ONS? COME OFF IT

BECAUSE IT'S NOT ALWAYS LOVE AT FIRST SIGHT.

- I don't think they have enough beer in the barrel.

- You're making my stock plummet.

- Nice perfume. Must you marinate in it?

- I actually identify as asexual.

- I'm already dating three women right now, but if I ever wanted to date a fourth it would be you.

- My favourite sex position is the virgin: you stand there with your legs shut, waiting for the right person to come along.

- You can have my number as long as I can have yours – I work in telemarketing.

- I would tell you my name but I don't like being labelled.

- You came here with friends, right? You should go and find them.

I'D GIVE YOU MY NUMBER, BUT I DON'T HAVE A MOBILE. OR AN EMAIL ADDRESS. AND YOU DEFINITELY WON'T FIND ME ON TWITTER OR FACEBOOK.

DATING DISASTER

WHEN ONE EVENING IS MORE THAN ENOUGH.

- I have to leave, I think I left the dog on.

- You remind me of my sister.

- My wife gets angry if I stay out too late.

- This feels like the beginning of a really great friendship.

- If only I hadn't just enrolled in a monastery.

- Do you have a headache? No? It's OK, I have one.

- I'd love to see you again tomorrow but I've already made plans with Netflix and four cans of lager.

- Would you like to meet my last girlfriend? It's no problem, she's still chained up in my basement.

- My marriage has been arranged since I was five.

- No, thank *you* for letting me watch you constantly text all evening.

- Yes, let's just ignore everything I said. Let's just talk about you some more.

DING DING, ROUND ONE

THESE WILL EITHER STOP THE FIGHT OR MAKE IT TEN TIMES WORSE – YOUR CALL...

- Can we skip the fight and go straight to the make-up sex?

- This happens so often, it's a good job you're sexy when you're angry.

- That sounds exactly like something Hitler would say.

- I'd agree with you, but then we'd both be wrong.

- Before you tell me what I did wrong, you should first know that I don't care.

- Oh, sorry, I zoned out, were you still talking about that?

- You sound just like your mother.

- I hear you but I'm not listening.

- You're like a plunger – you like bringing up old crap.

- That sounds reasonable. Excuse me, time for my pills.

- Yes dear.

YOU'VE BEEN DUMPED

IT'S YOUR OWN FAULT FOR NOT SPOTTING THE SIGNS.

- If you need space, join NASA.

- I'm already visualising the duct tape over your mouth.

- It's such a relief that you're gay! You are gay, right?

- Warning: your message could not be sent. The Ex you're trying to contact has moved on. Error: 2 years wasted.

- I hope things don't get awkward between us, like they are right now.

- That's fine. Is your mother seeing anyone?

- Thank heavens for that, I feared any children we had would get your nose.

- I hate you, I'm just not in hate with you.

ENDING IT: LETTING THEM DOWN GENTLY

IT'S NOT YOU, IT'S ME.

- I just don't have time for a relationship right now.

- We just aren't in the same place.

- I need some space.

- My parents just got divorced 18 years ago, so I'm still a bit fragile.

- My psychotherapist thinks I should move on.

- I've decided to dedicate my life to finding out the truth about Princess Diana.

- Sorry, but Mum wants me to marry a Druid.

- Thank you for taking the time to participate in this social experiment.

- I'm moving to Antarctica tomorrow to start work on important governmental research.

I'M DYING. I CAN'T ASK YOU TO WATCH ME EBB AWAY. PLEASE, GO NOW AND REMEMBER ME AS I AM.

I DON'T THINK YOU'D STAY WITH ME IF I WAS DISFIGURED IN AN ACCIDENT, SO I'M LEAVING YOU NOW IN CASE IT HAPPENS.

ENDING IT:
PARTING BLOWS

IT'S NOT YOU – WELL, ACTUALLY IT IS.

- I just can't be with someone who likes *Magic Mike*.

- I don't believe in monogamy, so I think it's best I just spare you the heartache.

- The mothership has returned and I must leave. Pay no attention to my android double when you see it.

- I'm making some changes in my life. If you don't hear anything from me... you're one of them.

- I'm sure you'll make some guy that isn't me really, really happy some day.

- Marriage can be a fine institution, but I'm not ready for an institution.

- I really like you. So does my wife.

- This isn't working out. I think we should start making other people miserable.

- You call it a one night stand. I call it an audition.

- Marriage is not a word. It's a sentence.

ENDING IT: NUCLEAR OPTIONS

IT'S NOT YOU, IT'S YOUR HAIR. AND YOUR CLOTHES. AND YOUR PERSONALITY.

- Remember it's mind over matter. I don't mind and you don't matter.

- Word of the day is 'closure'.

- Here's the phone number of my doctor. I think you and he should talk.

- Oh, hi Lisa, er, Katie? Sally? Oh, yes now, Vicki, right? Tanya? Does it start with a 'T'?

- I will always cherish the initial misconceptions I had about you.

- Sometimes I think I'd be better off dead. No, wait, not me, you.

- I hate being pissed off, but with you, it comes so naturally.

- Welcome to Singletown. Population: you.

- It's been lovely but I have to scream now.

- It was love at first sight. Then I took a second look.

I DON'T
THINK WE'RE
COMPATIBLE.
YOU'RE A
TYPICAL ARIES
AND I THINK STAR
SIGNS ARE A
LOAD OF BS.

DO YOU THINK
THE CEILING
NEEDS PAINTING?
(ALL IN THE
TIMING...)

TURN BACK TIME?

NO, WHEN IT'S OVER, IT'S OVER.

- I have finished my unfinished business with you.

- How much are you willing to pay me?

- You looked better when I was drinking.

- If your phone doesn't ring, that will be me.

- I think we should just be friends with sexual tension.

- I'm just a reminder of what you can't have.

- I'll be your sex object – every time you ask for sex, I'll object.

- Roses are red, violets are blue, I'm happy to know, I can live without you.

- As it turns out, moving on without you in my life was much easier than I thought.

- People say you don't know what you have until you lose it. I know. Blimey, I know…

- You always said that you would die for me. Now that we've split up, I think you should keep up your end of the deal.

- I've missed you, but my aim is getting better.

- Let me know when you're available so I can make sure I'm busy.

- No calls I understand. No texts I understand. When you see me with someone else I hope you can understand.

- Yes, I'm smiling, but you're not the reason anymore.

- What I like best about our relationship is that you're no longer in it.

'I LOVE YOU'

WHEN YOU DIDN'T WANT TO HEAR THOSE THREE LITTLE WORDS.

- Who doesn't?

- If only there was someone who loved you.

- If only I could get your friend to say that.

- Already? Damn I'm good.

- I love beer.

- I get that a lot.

- I know, you told me yesterday.

PROBLEMATIC PEOPLE

THE BEST

THERE ARE SOME PEOPLE IN LIFE
THAT ARE SENT TO TRY US.

They may be our friends, well-meaning strangers or just people doing their job, but the bit of them that should monitor self-awareness never seems to work. The problem comes at that moment when they cross the line between 'friendly' or 'helpful' and 'downright annoying' – it seems perfectly obvious to us but not to them.

That's where the right brush-off is essential. They'll get the hint (or, depending on your choice, a massive neon sign) that your time with them is up and they should move on.

It might not be their fault, though. You clearly have such a magnetic personality that all types are drawn to you and want to be around you as long as possible. Then again, they might just be idiots...

CHEATING THE CHUGGERS

CHARITY BEGINS IN SOMEONE ELSE'S HOME.

- Yes I am interested to hear more about unwanted cats – they go great in a bhuna.

- Sorry, I thought you were giving money to me.

- I gave all my spare cash to the pub.

- If someone dies of malnutrition every time you click your fingers STOP CLICKING YOUR FINGERS.

- I'm in a hurry to be anywhere else.

- If you believe in this cause so passionately, why are you paid to collect for it?

- Of course, I love the WWF! Stone Cold Steve Austin, The Rock, yes. Poor souls. Not much money in wrestling any more?

- Sorry, I thought you were a clipboard salesman.

CAROL MINGERS

IF PEOPLE STOOD ON YOUR DOORSTEP SINGING AND DEMANDING MONEY AT ANY OTHER TIME OF YEAR YOU'D CALL THE POLICE.

- Stop singing about figgy pudding – I'm gluten intolerant.

- You can't see three ships, we're fifty miles from the coast.

- Please stop torturing the cat.

- I'm deaf, but I can still tell you're off key.

- Do you do requests? How about 'A million green bottles'?

- Shhh, my hamster is meditating.

- I wrote that carol, you owe me royalties.

- I'm calling Trading Standards – this is not a 'Silent Night'.

SHOP FLOOR FOOLS

IT'S LIKE THEY WANT YOU TO BUY EVERYTHING OVER THE INTERNET.

- Please ask me again after I've been in the shop more than five seconds.

- You *can* help – does the rash on my back look inflamed?

- Yes, I'm having a lot of trouble finding the thing that is right in front of me.

- Actually, you can help. I'm looking for enriched uranium, a goat carcass and a picture of your mum.

- Yes, I do want advice from someone with no training who gets paid on commission.

- I do have a question about it – which website sells it the cheapest, Amazon or eBay?

- No thank you, if I wanted a chocolate orange, a bar of chocolate, a chocolate bunny, a bag of chocolates, a box of chocolates or some chocolatey chocko chocky-choc chocolate, it would be in my basket.

- I'll sign up to your email newsletter if you sign up to mine. It's called 'SILF' – the 'S' is for salespeople.

- Are you selling me a warranty because you know my purchase will break down in four months?

WACKY WAITERS

JUST DON'T USE ANY OF THESE LINES BEFORE YOUR FOOD ARRIVES.

- I'm enjoying my meal the same amount as I was two minutes ago.

- How did I find the beef? It was under a carrot.

- No dessert thank you, my arteries are still screaming from the main.

- If you draw a smiley face on my bill, I'll know you love me.

- So, how's the acting career going?

- If you ask me if I want a dessert for a third time, do I get it for free?

- A table for how many? Well clearly one as my girlfriend can sit on my shoulders.

ICE-COLD CALLERS

THEY ARE TRAINED TO NOT HANG UP. YOU'LL NEED YOUR A-GAME HERE.

- I know you're just doing your job. Perhaps you should get a better one.

- I am the managing director of your company.

- How did you get my number?

- I'm busy right now. Please give me your home number and I'll call you back later.

- Do I need a loan? Why yes, I've just filed for bankruptcy, so you couldn't have timed it better.

- What are you wearing?

- Dave? Is that you? Dave, how have you been? Wow, it's been ages.

- Will you be my friend?

- Sorry, I'm hard of hearing – please speak louder... louder... a bit louder...

- Please talk very slowly, because I want to write down every wonderful word you say.

DODGY DEBTORS

YOU MIGHT OWE THEM MONEY, BUT NOTHING ELSE.

- I think you're just too wrapped up in the whole concept of 'money'.

- So, you're talking to me because the rent's not paid? Is that all I am to you? A tenant?

- I can't afford next month's rent, so why bother with this month's?

- Don't tell anyone, but I'm going into the witness protection programme.

- I'm low on cash – my dealer raised his prices again.

- Paying rent every month is boring – I don't want my life to be soooo predictable.

- I'm on house arrest so I can't get a decent job.

ON AND ON AND ON AND ON

WHEN THERE ARE NOT ENOUGH HOURS IN THE DAY.

- Do you ever get cramp in your tongue?

- So what happen in the final episode of this thrilling anecdote?

- You remind me of my Uncle Geoff. He's really boring as well.

- What do you actually do, besides talking?

- Can we head to the final instalment?

- There was a time when I would've held a strong interest in the words you speak. I think of it fondly.

- Sorry, I'm getting a call from someone. Anyone.

- Please cancel my subscription to your podcast.

- You know I'm just going to forget all this anyway?

- I am truly sorry I asked.

- When do you get to the good part?

WHO SHOULD I CALL
TO PAY THE RANSOM?

I WISH CONVERSATIONS
WERE LIKE USER
AGREEMENTS WHERE
I COULD SKIP TO THE
END AND JUST AGREE.

NO, I ALWAYS YAWN
WHEN I AM INTERESTED.

MY HOPE FOR YOU IS
THAT YOU SOMEDAY
FIND THE END OF YOUR
SENTENCE.

OVERSTAYING OAFS

HOW BIG A HINT DO YOUR GUESTS NEED?

- Please do come again when you can't stay so long.

- Sorry to see you are leaving at last.

- Let me get your coat.

- Can I get you anything? A coffee, a biscuit, a lift home?

- Can you leave now, we want to have sex.

- I'm just going to throw away my welcome mat.

- You have delighted us long enough.

- I don't want to keep you.

- My bandwidth limit is exceeded.

- So, where are you heading in five minutes' time?

- Would you like a cup of tea before heading off immediately afterwards?

- Your visits always give pleasure – if not the arrival, the departure.

SPARE-ROOM SQUATTERS

THEY SAID IT WOULD ONLY BE FOR A COUPLE OF NIGHTS...

- I think it's time we discussed your share of the bills.

- How would you like your room decorated?

- Can you give a me a hand cleaning the septic tank?

- I had a dream last night that I killed you.

- Are you too good for your own home?

- I know you're gluten intolerant, but my doctor has ordered me to start a gluten-only diet.

- Let's share our favourite quotes. Mine is by Benjamin Franklin: 'Fish and house guests smell after three days.'

- My second favourite quote is by me: 'Get the hell out of my house.'

CUTTING COMMS

IN THE OLD DAYS IT WASN'T THAT CONVENIENT TO BRUSH SOMEONE OFF WITH A WITTY COMEBACK OR SARCASTIC REMARK. HOW UNCOMFORTABLE MUST IT HAVE BEEN TO DICTATE #SMARTARSE TO THE POLITE TELEGRAPH OPERATOR? WHAT WAS THE PATTERN FOR A YAWNING EMOJI IN SEMAPHORE? HOW LONG DID IT TAKE TO SHAPE A MIDDLE FINGER IN SMOKE SIGNALS?

Things started getting easier when it became possible to fax a picture of your bottom to head office.

But now we have the opposite problem. With so many communication channels open to us and so many people demanding our attention, we need ways to stem the tide of unnecessary chatter.

You do have to bear in mind that a lot of communication methods are public. This cuts both ways. The right brush-off will send a message far and wide. The wrong one will make you tomorrow's meme.

NO ANSWER

AFTER THE BEEP, PLEASE DON'T LEAVE A MESSAGE.

- There is a 99% chance I am screening your call.

- If you are not an international supermodel wanting company or offering me at least £100,000 no questions asked, please hang up now.

- If this is the police, the tax office or my mother, you have the wrong number.

- You have five seconds to capture my interest. Go!

- Thank you for reporting your location to the Axis of Evil headquarters. The nearest hit squad has been dispatched. Have a nice day!

- Congratulations winner! Yours is the 1000th call I have chosen to ignore!

- This is a telepathic thought-recording service. After the tone, think about your name, your number and your reason for calling, and I'll think about returning your call.

NO, YOU HANG UP

SHOULD YOU FORGET TO FILTER THE CALL.

- You have the wrong number.

- I'm just the babysitter.

- Sorry, I'm deaf in my left ear. Nope, sorry, still can't hear you – my right ear isn't that great either.

- I bought this phone number on eBay.

- That sounds like my number, but mine starts with a silent 7.

- Who? No, I'm not him. I'm my neighbour.

- You have me mixed up with some other guy with the same name and address.

- You're looking for my father. He died yesterday.

- I've just been shot by an intruder. I'm losing blood quickly. Can you call back later?

ANTI-SOCIAL MEDIA

BECAUSE YOU WANT TO CLEAR YOUR FEED FOR MORE PICTURES OF CATS.

- It must be difficult to post inspirational Tweets when your blood type is B Negative.

- I can't tell – is that a Monet painting or another photo of your spaghetti carbonara?

- Was that a Tweet or did your cat walk across your keyboard?

- If you deactivate your account, I'll 'Like' that.

- I would 'Like' all 400 of your back-to-school photos but I'd end up on a register.

- I'm not a Facebook status, you don't have to like me.

- Thanks to you I have learned that my prayers only get answered if I copy this post and make a wish within five minutes.

- I see the button for 'Like', but I don't see the one for 'Yawn'.

- #whatever

- Wow, if only all my stalkers were as bold as you!

I HOPE YOU GET A JOB SOON SO YOU CAN BORE PEOPLE ON LINKEDIN INSTEAD.

UNFRIEND? IS THAT IT? IS THERE NO 'UNMEET' BUTTON?

I WANTED TO THANK YOU PERSONALLY FOR THE 'LIKE'. THAT'S WHY I'M IN YOUR HOUSE.

ATTENTION-SEEKING MISSILE

WHEN THEIR ONLINE DRAMA IS NOT YOUR CRISIS.

- Your personal drama credit card has exceeded its limit.

- Thank you for the invitation to your pity party, but I'm busy.

- Would you like some cheese with that whine?

- Nobody is interested in your sorrow, unless you can make a joke or a poem out of it.

- I've enjoyed just about as much of this as I can stand.

- Has a soap opera writer hijacked your account?

- Is your drama going to have an intermission soon?

- I'm dizzy from riding your emotional rollercoaster.

VEXED TEXT

QK TXT MSG REPLIES 2 SAVE YR THUMBS.

- Sorry, my dog ate your text message.

- Don't make me use UPPERCASE.

- Hello. I'm the person sitting opposite you.

- Sorry I didn't text you back, but my phone recognised your number.

- Your text responses are so slow I can't keep up.

- Not responding to your text doesn't mean I wanted 20 more.

- When did you train a monkey to use your phone?

- Congratulations on showing the extent of your ignorance in 160 characters.

YOU'D LOOK MORE INTELLIGENT ON THIS WEBSITE IF EVERY TIME YOU THINK OF SOMETHING STUPID TO SAY, YOU DIDN'T SAY IT.

DO NOT FEED THE TROLLS

THE BOTTOM HALF OF THE INTERNET IS A SCARY PLACE.

- I'm glad to see you're not letting your education get in the way of your ignorance.

- Stupidity is not a crime so you are free to go.

- He who laughs last thinks slowest.

- Keep on typing, someday you'll write something intelligent.

- Wise people think all they say, fools say all they think.

- Sit down, give your mind a rest – it obviously needs it.

- I'd like to see things from your point of view but I can't seem to get my head that far up my ass.

- I hate people who use big words just to make themselves look perspicacious.

- Couldn't fail to disagree with you less than I already don't.

OUR SURVEY SAYS

WHEN A WEBSITE DEMANDS YOUR OPINION, YOU COULD JUST CLICK THE LITTLE CROSS, OR...

- The first three seconds I saw your website it was great, then the survey appeared.

- Rubbish – no porn here at all.

- No understand, what is website?

- You have asked me how to improve your website. Happy to – I am an internet consultant so where should I send my invoice?

- I think your website would be better if you paid your taxes in the countries where you made your profits.

- I would visit your website more if all your products were free.

- First you must answer my question – 'What is the air-speed velocity of an unladen swallow?'

- I will not answer your questions without my lawyer present.

WEARENOTA MATCH.COM

BECAUSE IT'S NOT GOING TO HAPPEN. NOT EVEN VIRTUALLY.

- Next time, swipe left.

- Nothing to see here.

- I could do much better with much less effort.

- You don't have any better-looking friends, do you?

- Your profile describes my ideal partner – please can you introduce me to them?

- I'd love to see a film with you, but I've already seen them all.

- I am not that desperate and you are not that lucky.

- If only I had a clone with worse taste than me.

- You clicked on me by mistake, right?

- Thank you for helping me decide to cancel my subscription.

- Happy 10th birthday to your profile pic.

AWKWARD INTERACTIONS

SO YOU'RE HAVING A FUN TIME. IT MIGHT BE A FAMILY GET-TOGETHER, A CHEEKY DRINK WITH COLLEAGUES AFTER WORK OR AN IMPROMPTU BARBECUE WHEN A MATE FINDS SOMETHING THAT MIGHT BE MEAT IN THE BACK OF THEIR FREEZER. DRINKS ARE POURING, CONVERSATION IS FLOWING, IT'S SMILES ALL ROUND.

Then it happens. Out of the blue, someone asks one of 'those' questions.

Not 'How was the traffic?', 'Seen any good films recently?' or 'Why is the man who invests all your money called a broker?' No. The sort of question that should be banned from any event considered 'good times'.

It's nice that your friends and family care about your wellbeing. But once they shift gears into nosey, or even worse, thinly veiled criticism, something has to be done.

Choose your brush-off. Close them down.
Get back to guessing what meat it is.

WHY ARE YOU STILL SINGLE?

THE QUESTION BELOVED BY AUNTIES AND SMUG COUPLES.

- Because the love of my life is Taylor Swift and if I can't be with her, I don't really want to be with anyone else.

- Why *aren't* you single?

- I propose to everyone I meet but none of them has said 'yes' yet.

- All of my girlfriends are already married.

- Why would I make one girl miserable, when I can make so many women so happy?

- Because I've seen the horrors you've been dating.

- People are afraid of my ninja abilities.

- I prefer to have my screaming matches in the supermarket with strangers.

- Because of the restraining order. You need to step back 20 feet.

- I'm Batman.

- I'm just waiting for her to divorce you.

- I'm holding auditions at my place. Wear something sexy.

- I'm waiting for your daughter to turn 16.

- My mail order bride hasn't arrived yet.

WHY ARE YOU SO QUIET?

PERHAPS DON'T ANSWER AT ALL TO KEEP UP THE MYSTERY...

- Empty vessels make the most noise.

- I prefer to listen.

- Confidence is silence. Insecurity is loud.

- I'm not one for wasting words.

- I'm only quiet around the people I detest.

- I've been that way since the incident.

- I'm not quiet in bed.

- Oh, you can see me?

- No one plans a murder out loud.

- I'm trying to imagine you with a personality.

WHAT'S UP?

AND THEY'RE NOT EVEN A CARTOON RABBIT CHEWING A CARROT.

- A preposition.

- My patience.

- Your time for asking dumb questions.

- A type of quark.

- The direction denoted by Z in a 3-D coordinate system.

- A great Disney movie.

- Now that you're here, my blood pressure.

- Sorry, that's confidential.

- The probability of me replying with 'Nothing much'.

- The opposite of down. Do you have trouble with left and right as well?

- The sky.

- Inflation. My mortgage payments. In fact, everything but my salary.

- My middle finger should be.

SMILE – IT MIGHT NEVER HAPPEN!

BECAUSE YOU HAVE ONE OF THOSE FACES.

- It did – you're here.

- I will, as soon as you leave.

- Would you say that to Morrissey?

- I'm working out – it takes more muscles to frown than it does to smile.

- I'm psychic and I'm too upset about what's about to happen to you.

- It seems wrong to smile before I kill someone.

- I didn't want you to think I was laughing at your haircut.

- My face isn't here to entertain you.

- Botox.

- Smiling goes against everything I stand for.

- How would you like it if I told you what to do with your body?

- I've been in a bad mood for the last ten years.

WHAT ARE YOU DOING WITH YOUR LIFE?

YOU NEED TO CLOSE THIS DOWN BEFORE THEY PROPOSE A HORRIFIC ROADMAP FOR YOU.

- It's a surprise.

- Wrecking it.

- Trying to figure out the most efficient way to waste it.

- Studying for a degree in 'get off my back'.

- Whatever you didn't do.

- If I told you, I'd have to kill you.

- Secretly designing a kitten-drowning machine.

- Making the opposite choices to the ones you made.

- Do you want the honest answer or one that won't ruin your day?

- I could show you my internet history but you might go blind.

I'VE STARTED A NEW COMPANY. FOR £450 YOU CAN INVEST IN THE BOTTOM RUNG OF MY NEW PYRAMID SCHEME.

WHY ARE YOU SO LAZY?

I GUESS YOU'RE TOO LAZY TO THINK OF YOUR OWN BRUSH-OFF LINE.

- Hard work never killed anybody, but why take that chance?

- Being lazy is still ten times better than being you.

- I'm training for a *Game of Thrones* marathon.

- They say practice makes perfect. But nobody is perfect so I don't practise.

- I just rest before I get tired.

- You choose to call it lazy. I choose to call it selective participation.

- I'm not lazy... I'm just on my energy-saving mode.

- It might look like I'm doing nothing, but at a cellular level I'm really quite busy.

- I get enough exercise just pushing my luck.

ARE YOU SURE YOU WANT ANOTHER PINT?

WHY THE TATTLE ABOUT A LITTLE TIPPLE?

- I'm not an alcoholic. Alcoholics need a drink, but I already have one.

- A camel can work 10 days without drinking, I can drink 10 days without working.

- I used to drink all brands of beer. Now, I am older Budweiser.

- I'm only drinking to make you more interesting.

- According to chemistry, alcohol is a solution.

- I say 'no' to alcohol, it just doesn't listen.

- My drinking team has a darts problem.

- I'm not slurring, I'm speaking in cursive.

I WANTED TO LOSE 10 POUNDS THIS YEAR. ONLY 13 TO GO.

IT WOULDN'T BE FAIR TO EVERYONE IF I WERE THIS INTELLIGENT, FUNNY AND THIN.

I'M AFRAID OF HEIGHTS, NOT WIDTHS.

ARE YOU PUTTING ON A COUPLE OF POUNDS?

YOUR BODY IS A TEMPLE, BUT YOUR MOUTH IS AN ATHEIST.

- I'll start a diet as soon as the Christmas festivities are over.

- I'll start a diet when the Easter eggs are all gone.

- I'll start a diet when the summer barbecue season is over.

- I'll start a diet as soon as Massive Pie Year is over.

- I'm never going back to my original weight – 7lbs 6oz isn't very realistic.

- I have low blood sugar and dieting makes me dizzy.

- I'm not putting on weight, I'm just keeping up with inflation.

- I'm sure that arguing about going to the gym counts as resistance training.

ABOUT YOUR NEW TATTOO...

HOW CAN A LITTLE BIT OF INK START SO MANY QUESTIONS?

- Oh yes, it felt great when a 20-stone Goth jabbed a needle in my skin several thousand times.

- At least I chose this. Sorry the same can't be said about your personality.

- You're right, it's stupid, I should probably get it removed – just like your opinion.

- That was close, then, I nearly got it tattooed on you.

- My next one is of your face, or is that too ugly too?

- I got it while I was in jail for stabbing the last person that dissed my other tattoo.

INSERT PRYING QUESTION HERE

BECAUSE THEY ARE PLAIN OLD IN YOUR BUSINESS.

- I found your nose – it's in my business again.

- Remember when I asked for your opinion?
  Me neither.

- Oh, I didn't tell you? Then it must have been none of your business.

- Unless you're my bunched-up pants, don't be up my arse.

- Solve your own problems before you try to solve mine.

- Don't you have your own life to worry about?

- Stalk me on Facebook like a normal person.

- I've got five fingers. The middle one is for you.

- I'm sorry my life is more interesting than yours.

- I didn't realise you were an expert on my life and how I should live it. Please continue while I take notes.

- If I want your opinion, I'll ask you to fill out the necessary forms.

ON THE JOB

AH, THE DAILY GRIND. THE COAL FACE.
THE GRADUAL CRUSHING OF YOUR SOUL
VIA REPETITIVE MINDLESS TASKS EVEN A
MONKEY WOULD BE OVERQUALIFIED FOR.

Whatever you do to earn a living, there are some people who seem determined to encroach on your working day. Whether it's your boss demanding results, your colleagues requesting help or your customers asking for anything at all, they never seem to understand that your current game of Candy Crush Saga is crucial.

A well-chosen brush-off will get your day back in order. However, a few too many and you might end up looking for another job.

As for interviews... no one enjoys being interviewed, especially if all the questions were first asked by Noah when he was choosing animals for positions on the ark. The right brush-off here will certainly have the interviewer searching for another question. Or, more likely, another candidate.

And please, have an adequate day.

OUT-OF-OFFICE EXPERIENCE

SET YOUR AUTO REPLY SO THEY DON'T EVEN TRY TO EMAIL A SECOND TIME.

- Please be assured that I am 100% on holiday and not using the out-of-office message as a way to avoid doing any work.

- Thank you for your email. Your credit card has been charged £3.99 for the first ten words and £1.99 for each additional word in your message.

- When you go on holiday, you can ignore my emails too.

- Your email is now filed alongside offers of Viagra and Russian brides.

- Please picture me enjoying a cocktail on the beach while you sit in a stuffy office.

- Your email has now been forwarded to the office junior who will pretend he never saw it.

- I will definitely look at your email the second I get back to the office. Definitely.

- Feel free to check out my Instagram feed to see how much more fun my life is than yours.

- At least you have a reply. If I were in the office, you'd be unlikely to get one at all.

- I will be back in the office on Monday and hope that my hangover will be gone by Wednesday.

- One of our trained monkeys will be in touch soon to answer your banal question.

WHERE DO YOU SEE YOURSELF IN FIVE YEARS?

NOT WORKING HERE.

- Celebrating the fifth anniversary of you asking me this question.

- Maybe a few feet to the right.

- Either dead or in prison.

- I don't know, my time machine is broken.

- I'll either happily be working here or winning *X Factor.*

- Cruising in my new yacht once I've sold your secrets to Google.

LATE AGAIN

**IF THE JOB WAS MORE INTERESTING,
YOU MIGHT BE ON TIME.**

- I tried a new way in to work. Don't worry, I won't be trying it again.

- I was too busy sleeping to be on time.

- Your watch must be fast.

- But this is the earliest I've ever been late.

- I have transient amnesia and I couldn't remember my job.

- I drove to the place I'd rather work at by mistake.

- I've had one too many sick days so I'm calling in dead.

- Do you know how long it takes to buy a *Big Issue* from every seller between the station and the office?

VAUNTED VOICEMAILS

IT'S NOT LIKE THEY EXPECT YOU TO CALL BACK.

- I am currently at a job interview and will reply to you if it does not go well.

- I am buying several last-minute lottery tickets and hoping never to return.
  Unfortunately, I will be back tomorrow.

- I am currently doing something far more important than taking your call.

- Please leave a message after the beep and I will treat it with the disdain it deserves.

- Feel free to guess my mobile number. Clue – it starts with a zero.

- I am visiting 1873 and voicemail has yet to be invented.

- Rest assured your messages will be deleted in the order they were received.

CUSTOMER DIS-SERVICE

BECAUSE CUSTOMER AND CLIENT ENQUIRIES REALLY GET IN THE WAY OF PROPER WORK (E.G. YOUTUBE).

- That's an issue for the delivery company.
- Sorry, the computer is on the blink.
- I'm new.
- Try looking on our website.
- Are you having a bad day too?
- The Data Protection Act says I can't do that.
- There's nothing I can do, it's company policy.
- Call back next week – they're replacing me with a computer.
- Ah, you need to speak to Geoff. He's on holiday.
- My supervisor is not available. He's on holiday too.
- My manager is also on holiday.
- In fact, I'm the only person not on holiday.

STOCK ANSWERS

YOU MIGHT HAVE ONE IN THE STOCK ROOM, BUT THAT MEANS LOOKING FOR IT.

- The last one just went.

- There's no call for that one round here.

- It was outlawed in 2003.

- We should get one in next week.

- They don't make that one any more.

- The supplier forgot to include them in our last order.

- We do have one, but it's held on reserve.

- To be honest, that one's rubbish. Try Amazon.

IT'S A THANKLESS JOB, BUT I'VE GOT A LOT OF KARMA TO BURN OFF.

I THOUGHT I WANTED A CAREER; TURNS OUT I JUST WANTED A SALARY.

TURNING DOWN TASKS

NOTE THAT SAYING ANY OF THESE TO YOUR BOSS MIGHT BE CONSIDERED AS YOUR RESIGNATION.

- I didn't see 'fixing your mistakes' in my job description.

- Your boss gave me something more important to do.

- Your email about it didn't pass the 'idiot' filter.

- Sorry, I fell asleep before you got to the point.

- Your platitude won't change my attitude.

- You didn't say I had to be on time every day.

- I'm not coming into work today. My brain is full.

- I said I needed some more training on the meat slicer.

- I don't work here. I'm a consultant.

- I have plenty of talent and vision; I just don't give a damn.

- I'm afraid the only service I can offer you is sarcasm.

IDIOTIC INTERVIEWERS

IT'S CLEARLY NOT THE JOB FOR YOU, SO END THE INTERVIEW AT ANY COST.

- I don't need five words to describe myself, two will do – lone wolf.

- In three years' time? Probably in your chair asking the questions.

- I was fired for using offensive language with a client.

- I wasn't aware that she was my manager's wife.

- I have motivational skills – everyone says they have to work twice as hard when I'm around.

- There is no address on my CV because I'm living in my car.

- I don't mind moving here as long as there are some nice restaurants and a couple of good strip clubs.

- I'm saving that information as a surprise for the second interview.

- I'd appreciate it if you actually listened to me rather than just take notes.

I DON'T NEED TO TAKE THE EARPHONES OFF – THE VOLUME ON MY iPHONE IS LOW SO I CAN HEAR BOTH THE SONG AND YOU.

WHAT IS YOUR BIGGEST WEAKNESS?

WHEN THE INTERVIEWER'S BIGGEST WEAKNESS IS ORIGINALITY.

- I can't resist giving smartarse answers to stupid questions.

- I have difficulty getting along with co-workers. And management. And customers.

- I have so many, it's hard to pick just one.

- Stealing as many office supplies as I can fit in my pockets.

- Weaknesses? Me? Are you nuts?

- Punching incompetent bosses.

- When I get bored I set fire to photocopiers.

- I hate change. And deadlines. And work. And your tie.

- I have a tendency to annex the Sudetenland.

DO YOU HAVE ANY QUESTIONS?

A WELL-TIMED QUESTION CAN BRUSH OFF AN INTERVIEWER TOO.

- Are all the staff as cute as you?

- I'm thirsty, could you get me a beer please?

- I'm a busy guy, can we wrap this up?

- Do you mind if I take my shoes off?

- If my drug test is positive, can I come back in a week's time to take it again?

- How far back do the criminal background checks go?

- Am I in the right room?

- Can I use my last two parole officers as references?

- When do I get to meet the important people in the decision-making process?

IDIOTS ABROAD

HOLIDAYS ARE MEANT TO BE A TIME TO
RELAX. THE FEW DAYS A YEAR YOU GET
TO KICK BACK FROM WORK AND
GET AWAY FROM IT ALL.

But the one thing you can't escape is people.

Unless, that is, you holiday alone on Mars, but that's unlikely unless you are a rich recluse reading this book in AD 2132. What's it like in 2132? Do we have jetpacks yet?

We hope you enjoy your holiday, wherever and whenever it is. If all else fails, just fire up a translation app on your phone that loudly repeats the Spanish for 'No more sangria please'. It works especially well in Japan.

Note – if you are wondering, we had some killer one-liners to drop on passport control, airport security and customs officers. But when our official brush-off tester tried them out he ended up in a Thai jail with no chance of parole.

A WING AND A PRAYER

WHAT YOU DIDN'T BUDGET FOR WITH BUDGET AIRLINES.

- Thank you for the offer of a meal, but I brought my own tasty bit of cardboard.

- I don't want to pay the excess luggage charge – let me remove the second feather from my luggage.

- Does the headphone rental charge include fumigation?

- No extra pillow thanks – I fear rubbing two of them together might create a spark and ignite whatever this guy next to me is emitting.

- Do the life jackets need a credit card to make them work as well?

- I would pay for a seat reservation, but I already sold a kidney to cover the check-in fee.

- The legroom is fine – I've always considered blood circulation a luxury.

- I will fly with you again – if all the other airlines close down.

- Please give my regards to rest of the cabin crew, the pilot and the stag party for making this an unforgettable flight.

DUTY FREEZE

THE SHOP WHERE 'NO TAX' AND 'NO TASTE' COLLIDE.

No thank you, I do not want to buy:

- enough cigarettes to give Eritrea emphysema.

- enough chocolates to make Denmark diabetic.

- enough bling to dazzle Dominica.

- enough souvenirs to sink Cyprus.

- enough perfume to make Singapore smell like my grandmother.

- enough vodka to make Malta think it is Russia.

CABIN PRESSURE

HOW ANNOYING CAN A PERSON BE IF THEY ARE STRAPPED INTO THE SEAT NEXT TO YOU FOR FOUR HOURS?

- Can you tell me where you got your elbow sharpener from?

- Please don't interrupt me while I'm trying to ignore you.

- It's OK, getting up twenty-seven times to let you out to the toilet will stop me getting deep vein thrombosis.

- There's nothing to worry about if you can't swim. If the plane crashes we'll most likely die on impact anyway. Can I borrow your magazine?

- Please can you turn your music up, I can only hear all of it?

- No, I didn't fart. I just blew you a kiss with my bottom.

- I can see your children enjoy playing in the aisle. Do you think they'd have more fun playing in the clouds?

- I once saw a piece of carry-on luggage larger than yours. They used it to pack New Zealand.

SIDESTEP THE REP

WHEN THE HOLIDAY REP'S ENTHUSIASM IS NOT INFECTIOUS.

- Oh, I get it. Like a joke, but different.

- I've had fun before. This isn't it.

- A sing-song is a great idea. If you are six.

- Are you paid to be like this or have you forgotten your medication?

- I didn't say this lousy hotel was your fault, I just said I was blaming you.

- Let me think, a quiet afternoon on the beach or white-water rafting with a bunch of sex-crazed drunks? Tricky choice. I'll get back to you next month.

- Thanks for the drinks vouchers. I'll need a few to help forget that coach ride.

- Sorry, I'm allergic to pink cowboy hats.

- You should get a job with Club Dead.

- I would go on the trip to the local folk craft market tomorrow, but I thought I'd count the grains of sand on the beach instead.

HOLIDAY CRASHERS

BECAUSE YOU DON'T SUFFER FOOLS ON HOLIDAY EITHER.

- I'm on holiday right now, but I would be happy to ignore you some other time.

- Today is not your day. Tomorrow is not looking good either.

- Did you come on holiday to give your family a week off?

- Keep talking, I'm diagnosing you.

- Enjoy the coach trip around the cliffs tomorrow. I just hope I don't tamper with the brakes in my sleep again.

- Sorry, I work here and I'm not allowed to fraternise with the customers. My uniform? It's casual Thursday.

- I'm having an introvert party in my hotel room later and you're all not invited.

- Who me? I just wander from room to room.

- I would join you for a drink in the bar, but the olives talk about me behind my back.

HAVE A
NICE DAY!

**IT SEEMS THAT THIS PHRASE COMES ON
HOLIDAY WITH YOU.**

- Don't tell me what to do.

- This one is already screwed. Can I save it
  for tomorrow?

- I'll have a nice day when I'm good and ready.

- Too late!

- Well, I do have a plan for a crappy day –
  I'll see what I can do.

- Your wife always makes sure I do.

- As opposed to what?

- I don't tell you how to live your life.

- I wish I'd thought of that. Thanks.

NO TIME FOR TIMESHARE

THE SALESPEOPLE THAT EVEN SALESPEOPLE AVOID.

- I like the idea of timeshare. How much would four seconds a year cost me?

- Three out of the four voices in my head think this is a bad idea. The other one wants me to paint you naked.

- The facts, although interesting, are irrelevant.

- Long term, this resort does not appeal to my polar bear fetish.

- I thought about investing in timeshare, but all my money is tied up in a chocolate teapot and inflatable dartboard start-up.

- Rather than us agreeing to disagree, why don't you just be quiet?

- I'll come here for two weeks every year if you live in my sock drawer for the rest of it.

- I'm not a proctologist, but I know an asshole when I see one.

- I already have a timeshare on the moon. It has more atmosphere than this place.

HOPELESS HAGGLING

THE STALLHOLDERS CAN SPOT A GULLIBLE TOURIST TEN MILES AWAY.

- The filter on my washing machine weaves a better rug than that.

- While 5 euros for a 'Rolox' watch seems like a great deal, I think I'll stick with my broken egg timer.

- Why do these traditional, handmade carvings have a 'Manufactured in Korea' sticker on the bottom?

- If I showed this item to a police officer, would you make a happy face or a sad face?

- What is your after-sales care plan?

- Which is the best toy to choke a small child, this one or this one?

- If you can't tell me what meat it is, I'm not eating it.

- Thank you, but I haven't had a tetanus booster for some years.

BROAD STROKE BRUSH-OFFS

IT'S NOT TOO MUCH TO ASK IS IT?
GETTING THROUGH A WHOLE DAY
WITHOUT SOMEONE BUGGING YOU?
UNFORTUNATELY, SCORING 24 HOURS
FOOL-FREE SEEMS TO BE INCREASINGLY
UNATTAINABLE.

For example, on how many occasions have you really needed someone to be quiet or go away? And that person who needed silencing or dispatching, were they the sort that needed telling more than once?

Of course, the best thing to do is avoid such situations in the first place. The right brush-off is the best response when you are invited to an event located within the seventh layer of hell.

We hope that this last selection of one-liners will be of assistance whatever the occasion. If they aren't, well, we would still like to help you out. So, which way did you come in?

WHO CARES?

BECAUSE CARING WAS NOT ON TODAY'S TO-DO LIST.

- Not my circus, not my monkeys.

- Not my chair, not my problem

- Who paid for this floor? Not me.

- Not my job, not my prob.

- I want you to know someone cares. Not me, but someone.

- I'd like to tell you I care, but I don't like to lie.

- Nobody cares as much as I don't.

- If I were Jay Z, your issue would be number 100.

- OK. Moving on.

- A shortlist of things I don't give: jot, damn and monkeys.

- Really, you know what that sounds like? Not my problem!

JUST GO AWAY - NOW

WE'RE SURE YOU ALREADY KNOW ALL THE ONES ENDING IN 'OFF'.

- On your bike.

- Take a hike.

- Take a long walk off a short pier.

- Take a running jump.

- Go into space and take your helmet off.

- Go make toast in the bathtub.

- Go play in the traffic.

- Go headbutt a table saw.

- Go jump in the lake.

- Sling your hook.

- Hop it.

- Hit the bricks.

- Get out of my face.

- Walk west 'til your hat floats.

- Put an egg in your shoe and beat it.

JUST GO AWAY – WITH FLAIR

BECAUSE YOU CAN'T MIC-DROP WITH JUST 'GO AWAY'.

- I'm just drawing you a map so that when I tell you to go to hell, you will know exactly where to go.

- If I promise to miss you, will you go away?

- Have a nice day – somewhere else.

- How many times do I have to flush before you go away?

- Some cause happiness wherever they go. Others whenever they go.

- If I throw a stick, will you leave?

- Long walks are highly enjoyable. Why don't you take one now?

- Is it even possible to get lost intentionally? Wanna go and find out?

- The last train to Idiottown leaves in a minute – be on it.

- I cordially invite you to initiate auto-coitus.

JUST GO AWAY – MAKING IT UP

WHAT DO YOU MAKE OF IT?

- Make like a banana and split.

- Make like a missile and cruise.

- Make like a baby and head out.

- Make like a bowel and move.

- Make like a dog and flea.

- Make like a tree and leave.

- Make like Houdini and disappear.

- Make like an airplane and take off.

- Make like a drum and beat it.

- Make like a bee and buzz off.

- Make like stockings and run.

- Make like an amoeba and split.

- Make like a nut and bolt.

- Make like Michael Jackson and beat it.

- Make like a tyre and hit the road.

- Make like a hockey player and get the puck out of here.

OH SHUT UP

QUICK WAYS TO STOP THE LIPS FLAPPING.

- Shut your gob.

- Shut your pie hole.

- Shut your cake hole.

- Shut your beak.

- Shut your trap.

- Shut it.

- Zip it.

- Shh.

QUIET PLEASE

WHEN 'SHUT UP' ISN'T ENOUGH.

- Do you talk when you sleep?

- Where's the remote? I forgot to press mute.

- Do you have some Deep Heat? My ears ache.

- Can you pass my scalpel? I need to check your vocal cords.

- I like the sound of you not talking.

- You should introduce your lower lip to your upper lip.

- If you ran like your mouth you'd be in great shape.

- Can't hear you, keep talking.

UNINVITATION

WHEN A NIGHT OFF IS MORE ATTRACTIVE THAN A NIGHT OUT.

- I'm saving myself for a better party tomorrow night.

- My comfort zone looks upset. It doesn't seem right to leave it.

- Do I look like a people person?

- I would socialise, but it gets in the way of me staying home and doing what I want.

- My fortune teller advised against it.

- My dog has had a big fright and I don't want to leave him.

- I need the time to come up with an excuse why I won't visit my sister as well.

- Excuse me, I left my body in my other clothes.

- I'm expecting an unexpected family emergency.

- I'm working on my bucket list and your party is not on it.

- I spent my train fare on a lottery ticket. If I win, I'll come next week.

I PREFER TO
REMAIN AN
ENIGMA.

THE MAN ON
TELEVISION
TOLD ME TO
SAY TUNED.

MY CRAYONS
ALL MELTED
TOGETHER.

NO LIMITS

PLEASE, TAKE THIS NO FOR AN ANSWER.

- I would rather stick needles in my eyes. Or your eyes.

- What part of the word 'no' do you not understand?

- A 'yes' would be the slow withering death of my soul.

- I'm trying to see how long I can go without saying yes.

- I no longer do things that make me want to kill myself.

- I'd rather remove my own pancreas with a toothpick.

- I really want to, but the voices tell me I shouldn't.

- The short answer is no. The long answer is nooooooooooooooooooo.

ANYTHING ELSE

I MEAN IT, ABSOLUTELY ANYTHING ELSE AT ALL.

- I want to spend more time with my shredder.

- I'm building a pig from a kit.

- I did my own thing and now I've got to undo it.

- I'm in training to be a household pest.

- I'm attending the opening of an envelope.

- I'm converting my calendar watch from Julian to Gregorian.

- I have to fulfil my potential.

- I'm having all my plants neutered.

- I have to study for a blood test.

- I have to rotate my crops.

- I have to thaw some karate chops for dinner.

- I've been scheduled for a karma transplant.

- The monsters haven't turned blue yet, and I have to eat more dots.

SEVEN
DEADLY WINS

WHEN YOU NEED TO BRUSH OFF INVITATIONS FOR A WHOLE WEEK.

- On Monday I binge on my 'Paint Drying' box-set.

- Tuesday is my 'Advanced Brush-Off' class.

- I can't go out on Wednesday, it's against my newly founded religion.

- I have food poisoning every Thursday.

- Friday is my official 'Suffer no fools' day.

- Saturday's not a good day for me, I'll be tired after a busy week.

- Sunday's out. How about never? Is never good for you?

- Actually, I don't usually go out on days containing the letter 'y'.